Defining
MOMENTS
OVERCOMING CHALLENGES

Michael J. FOX

I Can Make a Difference!

by Sunita Apte

CONSULTANT
Thomas Leitch
University of Delaware

BEARPORT
PUBLISHING

New York, New York

Credits
Cover and title page, © Trapper Frank/Corbis Sygma; Page 4, © Sygma/Corbis; 5, © AP/Wide World Photos; 6, © Sygma/Corbis; 7, © Time Life Pictures/DMI//Getty Images; 8, © Classmates.com; 9, © Jeff Vinnick/Getty Images; 10, © Canadian Broadcasting Company; 11, © Courtesy of Burnaby South High School; 12, © CBS/Landov; 13, © Corbis; 14, © Pictorial Parade/Getty Images; 15, © Doug Menuez/Corbis; 16–17, © Universal Pictures/Photofest; 18, © Universal Studios/Getty Images/NewsCom; 19, © Robin Platzer/Time Life Pictures/Getty Images; 20, © Universal/Courtesy Everett; 21, © AP/Wide World Photos; 22, © ABC/Photofest; 23, © 2002 Kathy Hutchins/Hutchins Photo/NewsCom; 24, © 1998 American Broadcasting Company; 25, © John Cetrino/AP/Wide World Photos; 26, © Alex Wong/Newsmakers/Getty Images; 27, © 2004 Mitch Gerber/starmaxinc.com/NewsCom.

Publisher: Kenn Goin
Project Editor: Adam Siegel
Creative Director: Spencer Brinker
Photo Researcher: Marty Levick
Original Design: Fabia Wargin

Library of Congress Cataloging-in-Publication Data
Apte, Sunita.
  Michael J. Fox : I can make a difference! / by Sunita Apte.
    p. cm. — (Defining moments. Overcoming challenges)
  Includes bibliographical references and index.
  ISBN-13: 978-1-59716-269-2 (library binding)
  ISBN-10: 1-59716-269-8 (library binding)
  ISBN-13: 978-1-59716-297-5 (pbk.)
  ISBN-10: 1-59716-297-3 (pbk.)
  1. Fox, Michael J., 1961– 2. Actors—Canada—Biography—Juvenile literature.
3. Actors—United States—Biography—Juvenile literature. 4. Parkinson's disease—Patients—Canada—Biography—Juvenile literature. 5. Parkinson's disease—Patients—United States—Biography—Juvenile literature. I. Title. II. Series.

  PN2308.F69A68 2007
  790.4302'8092—dc22

                                    2006010802

For more information, write to Bearport Publishing Company, Inc., 101 Fifth Avenue, Suite 6R, New York, New York 10003. Printed in the United States of America.

10 9 8 7 6 5 4 3 2 1

Table of Contents

What's Going On?

In November of 1990, actor Michael J. Fox was filming a movie in Florida. One morning, when he woke up in his hotel room, Michael noticed something odd. His left pinkie finger was trembling. Michael tried to make it stop, but he couldn't. His pinkie kept on shaking. What was going on?

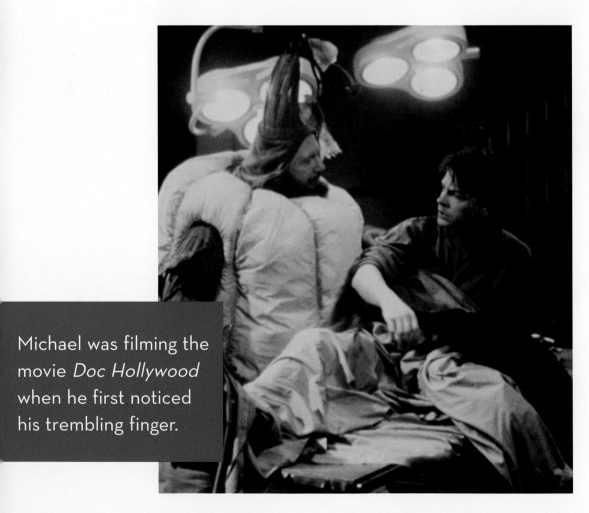

Michael was filming the movie *Doc Hollywood* when he first noticed his trembling finger.

Michael in a scene from Doc Hollywood

Michael shaking hands with fans in 1989, one year before his pinkie began twitching

Michael was a huge movie star. He was one of the most famous actors in America. Michael had already starred in a hit TV series and several **blockbuster** movies. His career seemed **unstoppable**.

A trembling pinkie wasn't going to change anything. Or was it?

Finding Out the Truth

Michael went to see a doctor in Florida, who said the trembling was not serious. Relieved, Michael finished filming his movie.

Yet the trembling didn't go away. In fact, it got worse. Finally, Michael could no longer ignore it. He **consulted** another doctor in 1991. The **diagnosis** he received shocked him. He had **Parkinson's disease**.

When people have Parkinson's disease, the brain cells that help control their body movements die. So they often have trembling hands, stiff muscles, slow body movements, and problems keeping their balance.

Michael has a form of Parkinson's disease that affects people under 40 years old. Most people who get Parkinson's are past 60.

Michael was confused. Parkinson's is a disease that usually strikes **elderly** people. He was only 30 years old. How could he have this disease, and what would it do to his career? Afraid, Michael decided to keep his illness a secret. He told only his family and close friends.

Michael's mother was one of the few people he told about his illness.

Destined for Fame

Michael Andrew Fox was born on June 9, 1961, in Edmonton, Alberta, Canada. His father was a sergeant in the Canadian Army. Like other military families, the Foxes moved around many times. Michael, his older brother, and his three sisters often had to make new friends. This was never a problem, however, for the smart and likable Michael.

Michael was very close to his grandmother, Nana. She predicted that he would "probably be very famous one day."

As a boy, Michael loved to write and illustrate stories.

Michael was always small for his age. He got teased about his size a lot, but he didn't let it bother him. Instead, he spent time doing things he loved, like playing hockey. Michael dreamed of becoming a **professional** hockey player.

Hockey is Canada's national winter sport. Michael's small size forced him to give up his dream of playing in the National Hockey League.

In Front of the Cameras

In junior high school, Michael discovered something else he loved to do—act. Michael was a good actor, too. He got his first big break when he was 16 years old.

Michael's acting teacher suggested that he try out for a Canadian TV series, *Leo & Me*. The part was for a 12-year-old boy, but Michael got the **role**. This time, his small size had helped him. By the next year, he was acting almost full-time. In fact, his acting was **interfering** with his schoolwork.

Michael in the 1977 Canadian TV series Leo & Me

So Michael made a big decision. He quit high school to concentrate on acting. When he was 18 years old, he moved to the center of the movie world—Hollywood.

Although he dropped out of high school, Michael still believed strongly in education. In 1994, he took a test to get a special high school diploma.

In 1995, a theater in Michael's hometown was named after him.

Hard Times in Hollywood

At first, Michael had no problem getting work in Hollywood. He landed a small movie role. He appeared in some TV shows. He even got a regular part in a TV series called *Palmerstown U.S.A.*

Michael (right) and the cast of Palmerstown U.S.A. *in 1980*

Michael added the "J." to his name after he got to Hollywood because there was already an actor named Michael Fox.

Michael's youthful looks meant he usually played someone younger than himself.

Success seemed easy, but life was about to teach Michael a lesson. *Palmerstown U.S.A.* was **canceled** after two seasons. Michael had trouble getting acting jobs. The bills started piling up. He began selling his furniture to make money.

Michael was thinking of moving back to Canada when the phone rang. A casting director wanted him to play a role in a new TV series.

A Big Hit

The new series, *Family Ties*, was a comedy about a family that had three kids. Michael would play the son, Alex P. Keaton. Unlike his parents and two sisters, Alex cared only about making money. Alex could have been an unlikable **character**, but Michael made him funny.

Michael with the Family Ties *cast. The show ran from 1982 to 1989.*

Michael won three Emmy Awards and a Golden Globe for his work on *Family Ties*. He became one of the most successful young actors in the country.

Michael winning an Emmy Award for **Family Ties**

The parents were supposed to be the stars of *Family Ties*, but audiences loved Alex the most. Soon, Alex became the show's main character. Michael became rich and famous. He bought a house and many cars. He signed autographs wherever he went. For the young actor, life had become a fairy tale.

A Lucky Break

While working on *Family Ties*, Michael heard about a film called *Back to the Future*. Michael wanted to play the main character in the movie, but it was already cast.

Then one day Michael got a call. The **producer** and director for *Back to the Future* weren't happy with the actor they had originally hired. A new star was needed. Would Michael do it?

The role of Marty McFly in Back to the Future *made Michael an international movie star.*

Michael jumped at the chance. He knew the movie would be great, and he was right. *Back to the Future* became a huge success. Now Michael was more famous than ever.

Back to the Future *was such a success that Michael made* Back to the Future Part II *(shown here)* and Back to the Future Part III.

Love and Marriage

The movie *Back to the Future* made Michael a huge star. Yet it was on the TV show *Family Ties* that he met his future wife.

The actress Tracy Pollan joined the show in 1985. She played Ellen, Alex Keaton's girlfriend. Tracy and Michael became good friends during that time. When Tracy finished shooting her **episodes**, she went back home to New York City.

The producers of *Family Ties* wanted Tracy to continue playing Ellen. She missed New York too much, however, and turned the offer down.

Tracy Pollan played Michael's girlfriend on TV and won his heart in real life.

Two years later, Michael was in New York making a movie. Tracy also had a part in the film. They began dating and got married in 1988. The next year their son, Sam, was born.

Michael and Tracy the year they were married

Keeping a Secret

Michael thought he had it all. He was rich and famous. He had a wonderful family. It seemed like nothing could go wrong. So when his pinkie trembled in the hotel room that morning in 1990, he mainly chose to ignore it.

Within six months, the twitch in Michael's pinkie had spread to his entire hand. Soon his shoulder became stiff as well.

Michael kept making movies after he knew he had Parkinson's. Here he is in a scene from the 1994 film Greedy.

Even after being diagnosed with Parkinson's in 1991, Michael tried to ignore the truth. He didn't see a doctor regularly. He didn't slow down and take it easy. Instead, he took medicine to stop his **tremors**. He learned to time the medicine so that it would stop his shaking just before he had to act. Michael could still keep his disease a secret.

Michael with his son, Sam, in 1995

Back to Television

In order to make movies, Michael sometimes had to fly to faraway places. He didn't like leaving his family behind. He also knew that the **hectic** pace of moviemaking was bad for his health. However, he wasn't ready to give up acting.

So Michael helped create a new television show. It would be filmed in New York City, where his family lived. *Spin City* went on the air in 1996, and it was an instant hit.

The cast of Spin City

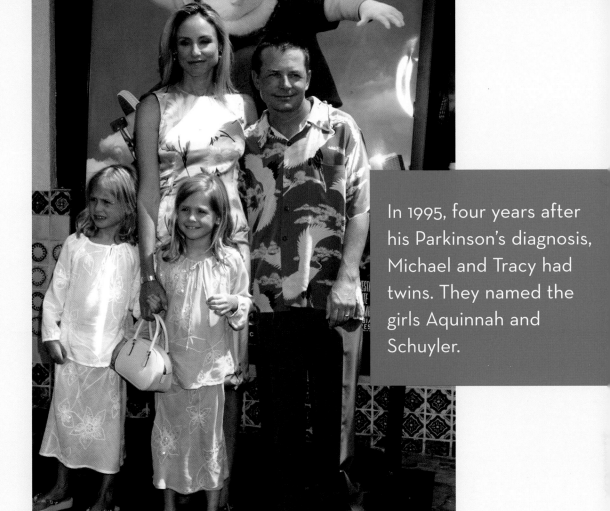

In 1995, four years after his Parkinson's diagnosis, Michael and Tracy had twins. They named the girls Aquinnah and Schuyler.

Michael with his wife and twin daughters

Still, there were problems. Like many television shows, *Spin City* was taped in front of a live audience. During taping, Michael had to work hard to control his tremors.

A Secret Revealed

Michael loved working on *Spin City*, but his Parkinson's was getting worse. He had brain surgery to stop the tremors on the left side of his body. Soon, however, tremors began on his right side. Within months he was worse than before. It was getting harder to hide his illness from the *Spin City* cast and crew. After seven years, the time had come to tell his secret.

While on *Spin City*, Michael often kept his hands in his pockets to hide their shaking.

Michael revealed his illness to the world during a TV interview with Barbara Walters in 1998.

Almost ten years after finding out he had Parkinson's, Michael still enjoyed playing hockey.

First, Michael told his coworkers about his illness. Then he talked about it in a magazine interview. Finally, he went on TV to discuss his disease. Michael was surprised by the **sympathy** and support people showed.

Making a Difference

In 2000, Michael quit *Spin City*. He wanted to spend more time with his family. Michael also believed that he could make a difference in finding a cure for Parkinson's. So that year he started the Michael J. Fox Foundation for Parkinson's Research. The organization's purpose is to educate people about the disease and raise research money.

Michael believes that a cure for Parkinson's can be found in his lifetime.

Michael has spoken to Congress about the need to spend more money on research for Parkinson's disease.

In 2001, Michael and Tracy had another baby daughter, Esmé. The entire Fox family is shown here, in 2004, with Esmé in front.

Michael considers himself a lucky man. He knows that life with Parkinson's is a struggle. Yet he believes that "the war against Parkinson's is a winnable war." Michael is determined to play a role in that victory.

Just the Facts

■ Though Michael gave up acting full-time, he has had recurring guest roles on several TV shows. He also does voices for animated films such as *Stuart Little*.

■ More than one million people in the United States are believed to have Parkinson's disease. As many as half of those people may not be diagnosed.

Timeline

Here are some important events in the life of Michael J. Fox.

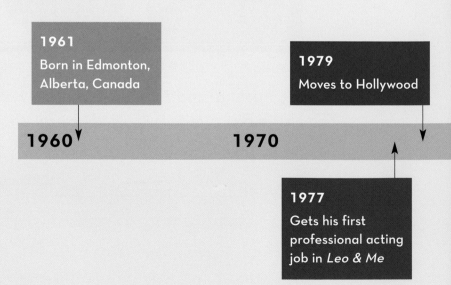

1961
Born in Edmonton, Alberta, Canada

1979
Moves to Hollywood

1960

1970

1977
Gets his first professional acting job in *Leo & Me*

■ When Michael's pinkie began to shake in 1990, he'd probably already had Parkinson's disease for five to ten years.

■ About 15 percent of the people who are diagnosed with Parkinson's are under 50 years old.

■ In 2002, Michael wrote a book about his life called *Lucky Man.* That same year, Michael got a star on the Hollywood Walk of Fame.

■ One of the most exciting nights of Michael's life was when he finally got to play hockey against his hero, hockey legend Bobby Orr.

1985
Stars in *Back to the Future*

1990
Notices trembling pinkie

1996
Stars in the TV show *Spin City*

2000
Leaves *Spin City* and establishes the Michael J. Fox Foundation for Parkinson's Research

1980   **1990**   **2000**   **2010**

1982
Appears on TV as Alex P. Keaton in *Family Ties*

1988
Marries Tracy Pollan

1991
Learns he has Parkinson's disease

1998
Has brain surgery and tells the public that he has Parkinson's disease

2002
Publishes *Lucky Man,* a book about living with Parkinson's disease

Glossary

blockbuster (BLOK-buhss-tur)
very popular or successful

canceled (KAN-suhld) for TV shows,
not being filmed anymore

character (KA-rik-tur) a person in a
book, movie, play, or TV show

consulted (kuhn-SUHLT-id) asked the
advice of

diagnosis (*dye*-uhg-NOH-sis)
the identification of a disease
or illness

elderly (EL-dur-lee) old

episodes (EP-uh-sohdz) shows that
make up a TV series

hectic (HEK-tik) busy, fast-paced

interfering (*in*-tur-FIHR-ing) getting in
the way of

Parkinson's disease (PARK-in-suhns
duh-ZEEZ) an illness in which brain
cells that help control body
movements die; this leads to
uncontrollable shaking, stiff muscles,
and slowness; at present, there is no
cure for Parkinson's disease

producer (pruh-DOOSS-ur) the person
who is in charge of raising the
money to make a TV show or movie
or put on a play

professional (pruh-FESH-uh-nuhl)
paid money to do something

role (ROHL) an acting part

sympathy (SIM-puh-thee)
the expression of concern for
someone else

tremors (TREM-urz) shaking of the
hands or other parts of the body

unstoppable (un-STOP-uh-buhl)
not able to be stopped

Bibliography

Fox, Michael J. *Lucky Man.* New York: Hyperion (2002).

www.cnn.com

www.michaeljfox.org

Read More

Ali, Rasheda. *I'll Hold Your Hand So You Won't Fall: A Child's Guide to Parkinson's Disease.* West Palm Beach, FL: Merit Publishing International (2005).

Bankston, John. *Michael J. Fox (Real-Life Reader Biography).* Hockessin, DE: Mitchell Lane Publishers (2002).

Kramer, Barbara. *Michael J. Fox: Courage for Life.* Berkeley Heights, NJ: Enslow Publishers (2005).

Wheeler, Jill C. *Michael J. Fox (Star Tracks).* Edina, MN: Abdo & Daughters (2001).

Learn More Online

Visit these Web sites to learn more about Michael J. Fox and Parkinson's disease:

http://faculty.washington.edu/chudler/mjf.html
www.michaeljfox.org/michael/

Index

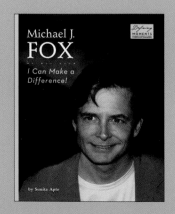

About the Author

A *Family Ties* fan, **SUNITA APTE** lives and writes in Brooklyn, New York. She writes both fiction and nonfiction for children and young adults.